Light And Darkness
By John C Burt

Walk in the light

There is no darkness in

The Light.

There is no darkness in

The Light.

There is no darkness in

The Light.

Light and Darkness

The Great Interplay

Light and Darkness
The Great Interplay
Always between
Light and Darkness.

Walk in the Light.
Walk in the Light.
Walk in the Light.
Walk in the Light.

Darkness has to Flee
When we choose
To walk in the Light.
I wanna make the

*Choice to Always
Walk in the Light.
I wanna make the
Choice to Always
Walk in the Light.*

**Because Darkness Has
To Flee When There
Is Light and the Light
Of Jesus is Present.**

**Because Darkness
Has to Flee When**

There is Light And
The Light of Jesus
Is Present.

May the Light of
Jesus Be Always
Present in My Life.
May the Light of
Jesus Be Always
Present in My Life.

The Light that will
And Can Dispel

All Darkness Is
Coming Again...
The Great Light of
The Son of God Is
Coming Again....
May He come quickly.
May He come quickly.
May He come quickly.

Where There Is The
Light of Jesus Christ
Darkness and evil cannot
Remain and Survive?
Light Forces Darkness

And evil to Flee, Flee
To Flee...

The Great Light of Jesus
Is Coming Again.
The Great Light of Jesus
Is Coming Again.
The Great Light of Jesus
Is Coming Again.
The Great Light of Jesus
Is Coming Again .....
Amen and Amen.

Fear And Faith
By John C Burt.

Fear Everybody Has
Some.
Fear Everybody Has
Some.
Fear Everybody Has
Some.
Fear Everybody Has
Some.

Faith In Jesus Deals
With the Fear Factor

In Our Lives.
Faith Forces Fear To Flee
In Jesus Name.
Faith Forces Fear To Flee
In Jesus Name.
Faith Forces fear To Flee
In Jesus Name.

Fear Of Man Is The
Greatest Fear We
Can Have...
So Do Not Be Afraid Of
Man And Humankind ..
Man Can Destroy The
Body And Hurt

*But They Cannot Change
Your Eternal Destiny.
Jesus Has Gone To
Prepare A Place for You,
A Home, A Home, A
Home, A Home.*

*Get Over The Fear Of
Man...Do Not Fear Man.
Cause Man is A Created
Being And Not
Almighty God.
Cause Man is A Created
Being And Not
Almighty God ...*

The Fear of The Lord
Is just the Beginning Of
Wisdom..
A Good Fear To
Possess.
A Good Fear To
Possess.

Yet it is Just The
Beginning Of The
Adventure With Jesus.
Which Is A Lifetime
Founded Upon A
Relationship With
Him.....

*The Adventure Of
A Lifetime Is What
Awaits Those Who Put
Fear To Death And
Put Their Faith In The
Man From Nazareth of
Galilee...*

*May He Be Honored
Forever. For He Is
Worthy To Be Honored,
Loved And Lifted High In
Our Lives ....*

Faith Deals With Our Fears For All Time. Replace Fear And Your Fears With Faith In The Man From Nazareth Out Of Galilee...

He Still Honors Faith In His Children ...
He Still Honors Faith In His Children .....
He Still Honors Faith In His Children ......

The Peace Of God.
By John C Burt.

There Is A Peace,
Called The Peace of
God ...
The Man from
Nazareth Out Of
Galilee said It Should
Guard My Heart From
The Darkness And
The Conflict In This
World...
Let It Guard Your
Heart ....

Let It Guard Your
Heart...
Let It Guard Your
Heart ....

Guard Your Heart
With The Peace Of
God ...
Guard Your Heart
With The Peace Of
God ...

The Peace Of God
Brings Peace, Welfare
And Wholeness ..

Jesus Through His Peace Makes Us Whole.

Jesus Through His Peace Makes Us Whole.

Jesus Is The Way Of Peace ...

He Is The Truth Of Peace ...

He Is The Life Of Peace ....

He Is A Peace That

Outlasts And Breaks
The Slavery And
Bondage Of Violence,
Hatred And War ....
His Peace Beats The
Sword Into Snowploughs
And Makes Them Useful ...

May The Prince Of Peace
Reign In Your Hearts,
Minds and Lives ....
May The Prince Of Peace
Reign In Your Hearts,
Minds and Lives ....
May He Reign Today ..

Amen, Amen , Amen

May The Prince Of

Peace All Peace

Come Again Soon ....

May The Prince Of

Peace All Peace

Come Again Soon ...

May The Prince Of

Peace All Peace

Come Again Soon ....

Amen and Amen ....

Son Of God , Son Of Man.
By John C Burt.

Messiah, Messiah, Messiah

Son Of God, Son Of Man

Son Of God, Son Of Man

Perfect Union, The God Man.

Perfect Union, The God Man.

Perfect Union, The God Man.

Perfect Union, The God Man.

Son Of God, Son Of Man .

Son Of God, Son Of Man .

Son Of God, Son Of Man.
Son Of God, Son Of Man.

The God Man From
Nazareth.
They believed Nothing
Good Could Come From
Nazareth.
How Wrong Could They
Be.
How Wrong Could They
Be.
How Wrong Could They
Be......

Son Of God, Son Of Man.
He Still Redeems People
Today.
Salvation Is His Business.
He Still Redeems People
Today.
He Still Redeems People
Today.....

He Came And Comes
To Seek The Blind, Lame,
The Outcast And Those On
The Fringes Of The
Community ...

He Loves To Be In The
Ditch With People..
He Loves To Lift People
Up....
He Loves To Lift People
Up........
He Loves To Lift People
Up ......

Son Of God, Son Of Man.
Son Of God, Son Of Man.
Son Of God, Son Of Man.
Son Of God, Son Of Man ....

Call Upon The Name
Of Jesus.
By John C Burt.

He Loves It When We
Call Upon His Name..
He Loves It When We
Call Upon His Name ....
He Loves It When We
Call Upon His Name....
He Loves It When We
Call Upon His Name ....

There Is Unlimited Power

And Authority Available
When His Name Is
Declared Over Situations.
Jesus Releases His Power,
Love and Authority Into
Situations When We Declare
It Over Them ....

Declare His Name.
Declare His Name..
Declare His Name ...
Declare His Name....
Declare His Name ...

His Name Tells You

His Character And
Who He is .....
His Name Tells You
His Character And
Who He is ......
His Name Tells Yo
His Character And
Who He is ....

Call Upon The Name Of
Jesus ...
Call Upon The Name Of
Jesus .....
Call Upon The Name Of
Jesus ....

So Call Upon The Name
Of Jesus And Be
Saved Today ....

So Call Upon The Name
Of Jesus And Be
Saved Today ......

So Call Upon The Name
Of Jesus And Be
Saved Today ....

Call Upon The Name Of
Jesus ....
Call Upon The Name Of
Jesus .....

Call Upon The Name
Of Jesus ....
Call Upon The Name
Of Jesus .....

He Loves It When We
His People Call Upon
His Name ....
He Loves It When We
His People Call Upon
His Name ....

So Call Upon His Name
Today, Today, Today ...
Today Is The Day of

Salvation ....

Today Is The Day Of

Salvation .....

Today Is The Day Of

Salvation ....

Son Of David.
 By John C Burt.

Son Of David. The
Coming And Reigning
King....
 The Son Of David.
 The Son Of David.
 The Son Of David.
 The Son Of David.

 The Coming And
 Reigning King...
 The Coming And

Reigning King...
The Coming And
Reigning King ....

The Son Of David Is
The King Of The Whole
World ....
The Son Of David Is
The King Of Creation ...

The Alpha And Omega.
The First And The Last.
He's The One Who Holds
All Things Together ....

So Rejoice In The
Son Of David The Great
I Am Today ...
So Rejoice In The
Son Of David The Great
I Am Today .....
So Rejoice In The
Son Of David The Great
I Am Today ....

The Son Of David
The Son of God
The Son Of Man
The Son Of David

The Son Of God

The Son Of Man

The Son Of David

The Son Of God

The Son Of Man ....

The Son Of David Came

Into The World Without A

Place To Sleep ....

The Son Of David Came

Into The World Without A

Place To Sleep ...

He Was Born Where

Animals Fed ...

He Was Born Where
Animals Fed ...

Such Humility For The
One Who Was The Son Of
David ...
The Son Of God
The Son Of Man
Such Humility For The
One Who Was The Son
Of David ..
The Son Of God
The Son Of Man

The Rightful King Of

Israel And The World
Created By The Word Of
His Father...

The Son Of David Rode
Into His City, The City Of
God, The Holy City,
Jerusalem On A Donkey.
Such Humility
Such Humility
Such Humility
The Son Of God
The Son Of Man
The Son Of David

The Rightful King Of
All Creation.
The Rightful King Of
All Creation.
The Rightful King Of
All Creation.

Riding Into His Father
God's Holy City of
Jerusalem On A
Donkey.
Such Humility
Such Humility
Such Humility
Such Humility.....

*Powerful In His
Weakness.
Powerful In His
Weakness.
Powerful In His
Weakness.*

*The Son Of David, The
Coming King, The Coming
King, The Coming King ....*

*The Son Of David
The Son Of God
The Son Of Man.
The Son Of David .....*

Prophet, Priest And King.
By John C Burt.

Prophet, Priest and King.

The Messiah Riding Into

The Holy City Of God

His Father On A

Donkey ......

Prophet,Priest and King.

The Messiah Riding Into

The Holy City Of God

His Father On A

Donkey ....

Prophet, Priest and King.
The Messiah Riding Into
The Holy City Of God
His Father On A
Donkey ....

Prophet The One
Who Declares The Word
Of The Lord To The
Nation Of Israel And
The Nations Of The World ...

Priest The One
Who Stands Before The
Father And Pleads For
And Represents The

People Belonging To
His Father God .....

King The One
Who Has All Authority,
Power And Dominion...

King The One
Who Has All Authority,
Power And Dominion ...

King The One
Who Has All Authority,
Power And Dominion ....

Prophet, Priest and King.

The Messiah Riding Into

The Holy City of God

His Father On A

Donkey ......

Prophet,Priest and King.

The Messiah Riding Into

The Holy City of God

His Father On A

Donkey ....

The Cross ...

By John C Burt.

The Cross

An Instrument Of

Torture And Pain

Inflicted Upon The

Lord Of All Creation.

Yet Jesus Willingly

Went To The Cross

For You And Me.

What A Wondrous

Cross.

What A Wondrous
Cross.
What A Wondrous
Cross.
What A Wondrous
Cross.

The Grace Of God
Shown And Won
Through The Cross
Of Jesus Christ....

The Grace Of God
Shown And Won
Through The Cross

Of Jesus Christ.

The Grace Of God
Shown And Won
Through The Cross
Of Jesus Christ ...

Its All About The Cross
Of Jesus Christ ....

Its All About The Cross
Of Jesus Christ .....

Its All About The Cross
Of Jesus Christ .....

The Most Amazing Event
In All Of Human History.
The Most Amazing Event
In All Of Human History.
The Most Amazing Event
In All Of Human History.

The Magnificent Cross
Of Jesus Christ....
The Magnificent Cross
Of Jesus Christ ......
The Magnificent Cross
Of Jesus Christ ....

The Cross, The Cross

The Cross, The Cross

The Cross, The Cross

Everything Revolves

Around And Finds

Its Definition In The

Cross Of Jesus Christ...

EPILOGUE :

Verse By Verse

Passion has all been about the Passion associated with knowing and being in relationship with Jesus Christ. The difference is that it has attempted to do this through verse by verse that hopefully evokes the passion, mystery and wonder of Jesus Christ. Thanks for reading this book and the verse by verse passion and prayerfully you have able to understand the passion and mystery and reflect on both?

.

Lightning Source UK Ltd.
Milton Keynes UK
UKHW051108060619
343922UK00003B/77/P